PROFESSIONAL INTELLIGENCE
EQ FOR WORKPLACE SUCCESS

OMRAN KHAYAMI

Copyright © 2024. All rights reserved.
No part of this book may be reproduced, distributed, or transmitted in any form or by any means, including photocopying, recording, or other electronic or mechanical methods, without the prior written permission of the author, except for brief excerpts in critical reviews or analyses.

Table of Contents

Preface: _____ *5*

Introduction _____ *7*

Chapter 1: Decoding Your Emotional Toolkit _____ *11*

Chapter 2: Strategies for Emotional Regulation _____ *19*

Chapter 3: Enhancing Communication with EQ _____ *25*

Chapter 4: Cultivating Emotional Resilience _____ *33*

Chapter 5: EQ for Leadership _____ *41*

Chapter 6: EQ in Team Dynamics _____ *49*

Chapter 7: Ethical Leadership and Decision-Making with EQ *57*

Chapter 8: The Future of EQ in Professional Development __ *65*

Chapter 9: Tools & Resources for Enhancing EQ _____ *73*

Conclusion: Mastering Professional Intelligence _____ *81*

Preface:

In a world where the professional demands on individuals grow increasingly complex, mastering emotional intelligence (EQ) is more critical than ever. "**Professional Intelligence: EQ for Workplace Success**" serves as a comprehensive guide to harnessing EQ to enhance your career success.

This book is crafted for those looking to improve their interpersonal skills within the workplace, from seasoned executives to those just beginning their careers. Here, you will find a blend of practical advice, grounded in research and real-life examples, aimed at helping you manage your emotions and better understand those of others.

Structured to walk you through the fundamental aspects of emotional intelligence, the book begins with self-awareness, advances through managing and influencing the emotions of others, and covers the application of EQ in leadership and teamwork. Each chapter builds on the previous one, supplemented with exercises and reflection points that encourage practical application of the concepts discussed.

Through real-life stories and actionable advice, this book aims to inspire you to integrate emotional intelligence into your daily professional interactions. As you delve into the chapters, you'll gain tools not only for professional advancement but also for personal growth.

Thank you for choosing to explore how EQ can redefine success in your professional life. I invite you to engage with this material actively, as we embark on this journey to harness the transformative power of emotional intelligence.

INTRODUCTION

Introduction

Welcome to "Professional Intelligence: EQ for Workplace Success," your essential guide to mastering the art of emotional intelligence (EQ) at work. This book isn't just a study; it's a practical toolkit designed to revolutionize the way you interact in your professional life. Whether you're just stepping into the workplace or steering a company, the secrets to career success often hinge not just on your smarts but on your ability to manage emotions—both yours and those of others around you.

EQ is about understanding your feelings and reactions and using this awareness to manage yourself and your relationships more effectively. It's crucial in every interaction at work, from negotiating deals to giving feedback, managing stress, and leading teams. High EQ helps you navigate the social complexities of the workplace, resolve conflicts, and lead with effectiveness. It's as essential as your cognitive intelligence (IQ) in predicting success, shaping not just professional outcomes but personal satisfaction too.

The Power of Emotional Intelligence

In this book, we unfold the layers of EQ, demonstrating its fundamental role in boosting your workplace dynamics and career trajectory. By enhancing your EQ, you'll find yourself able to wield greater influence, forge productive relationships, and cultivate a thriving professional environment.

But what exactly is EQ? It encompasses the skills to be aware of, control, and express one's emotions, and to handle interpersonal relationships judiciously and empathetically. This ability stretches beyond mere emotional awareness; it involves managing emotions constructively to relieve stress, communicate effectively, empathize with others, overcome challenges, and defuse conflicts.

Why EQ is Indispensable

Emotional intelligence is critical in today's work environments. It refines how we connect with colleagues, approach problem-solving, manage stressful scenarios, and lead people. For example, consider a project manager in Abu Dhabi whose high EQ allows him to inspire and guide his team through stressful project phases successfully, resulting in better outcomes and stronger team cohesion.

Your Roadmap Through This Book

"Professional Intelligence: EQ for Workplace Success" is meticulously structured to guide you step-by-step through the different facets of emotional intelligence. Each chapter builds upon the last, offering a progressive exploration of how to recognize, understand, regulate, and use emotions effectively in various professional settings. This book blends theoretical knowledge with practical tools, case studies, and actionable tips designed to empower you to harness EQ to your professional advantage.

As you navigate through these chapters, you'll encounter a blend of expert advice, practical exercises, and reflective questions that will deepen your understanding of EQ and enhance your ability to apply it in diverse professional scenarios. This structured approach ensures that you not only learn about EQ but also how to implement it effectively to see real improvements in your professional life.

Embarking on Your EQ Journey

This journey will transform your understanding of the workplace and your role within it. As you progress through this book, you'll gain a deeper appreciation of how emotions influence professional interactions and outcomes. By mastering EQ, you'll be equipped to handle challenges more effectively, lead with confidence, and create a positive impact in your professional environment.

This introduction sets the stage for a comprehensive exploration of EQ, preparing you for a journey of growth and professional development. Whether you are an aspiring professional, an established manager, or a seasoned executive, this book offers invaluable insights that will enhance your emotional intelligence and, consequently, your professional success.

1 DECODING YOUR EMOTIONAL TOOLKIT

Chapter 1: Decoding Your Emotional Toolkit

Understanding and Managing Your Emotions

Welcome to the first step of your EQ journey! This chapter is all about getting to grips with your own emotions and learning how to manage them in the workplace. Think of this as unpacking and understanding your emotional toolkit. Whether it's handling the rush of a tight deadline or navigating a tricky conversation with a coworker, knowing what tools you have and how to use them is crucial. Generally, there are 8 core emotions that we need to be aware of:

ANGER	FEAR	PAIN	SHAME
• Frustrated, Furious, Irritable, Mad, Resentful	• Anxious, Scared, Terrified, Threatened, Unsafe	• Grief or loss, Hurt, Lonely, Pity (self and others), Sad	• Ashamed, Disgraced, Embarrassed, Humiliated, Shameful
GUILT	**JOY**	**STRENGTH**	**LOVE**
• Guilty, Irredeemable, Regretful, Remorseful, Sorry	• Celebratory, Content, Grateful, Happy, Hopeful	• Confident, Fearless, Resilient, Safe, Strong	• Affectionate, caring, Connected, Longing, Passionate

Self-Awareness: The First Tool

It all starts with self-awareness. This means being tuned in to what you're feeling at any given moment. Are you stressed, excited, worried? Recognizing your emotional state is the first step in using it to your advantage rather than letting it control you.

For example, imagine you're a project manager who needs to deliver some tough feedback. By being aware of your emotions, you can approach this task in a way that is constructive rather than confrontational, ensuring your feedback is helpful and heard.

Techniques to Enhance Self-Awareness

Here are some practical ways to boost your self-awareness:

- **Emotional Journaling:** Spend a few minutes each day writing down what you felt at work and why. This can help you spot patterns and triggers in your emotional responses.
- **Mindfulness Practices:** Techniques like meditation can calm your mind and sharpen your focus, making it easier to observe your feelings throughout the day.

To see how these practices translate into real workplace scenarios, consider the story of Maryam, a customer service manager in the tech industry:

HARNESSING SELF-AWARENESS FOR CONFLICT RESOLUTION

Consider the experience of Maryam, a customer service manager at a tech company in Saudi. During a particularly heated meeting with her team, Maryam noticed her frustration beginning to rise as the discussion about a delayed product release became increasingly contentious. Recognizing her emotional state through the self-awareness practices she had honed—specifically, the emotional journaling she performed regularly—Maryam took a moment to breathe deeply and reframe her thoughts.

Instead of succumbing to her initial impulse to defend her team's decisions aggressively, she acknowledged her feelings internally and shifted her focus to understanding her team's diverse perspectives. This pause allowed her to approach the situation with a calm demeanor, acknowledging the stress the delay was causing everyone and emphasizing the team's shared goal of delivering a high-quality product. Her response not only defused the tension in the room but also encouraged a more collaborative problem-solving effort.

> This incident was a turning point for Maryam. It reinforced how vital her emotional self-awareness was not only in managing her reactions but also in leading her team effectively through stressful situations. This experience now serves as a cornerstone example Maryam shares with new managers during training sessions, illustrating the direct impact of emotional intelligence on leadership success.

Understanding Others' Emotions

Knowing your own emotions is half the battle; the other half is understanding those around you. This skill, called empathy, is invaluable in creating positive workplace relationships. It involves noticing and appreciating the feelings of others, whether it's spotting a teammate's frustration or recognizing a client's enthusiasm.

Empathy in Action: Why It Matters

Consider Layla, a team leader who notices one of her team members seems quieter than usual during meetings. By recognizing this change and gently asking if everything is okay, Layla can provide support that might help her teammate open up or resolve an issue that's been bothering them. This not only helps the individual but can also improve the team's overall dynamic.

Building Your Empathy Skills

Here's how you can start strengthening your empathy:

- **Active Listening:** Pay close attention to what people are saying and how they're saying it. This involves more than just hearing words; it's about understanding the emotion behind them.
- **Ask Open-Ended Questions:** Encourage people to express themselves more fully, which not only shows that you care

but also gives you better insight into their thoughts and feelings.

Emotional Triggers in the Workplace

Understanding what triggers emotional responses in you and others can help you manage reactions and maintain a professional environment. Common triggers might include tight deadlines, critical feedback, or overbearing workloads.

Navigating Emotional Triggers

Being aware of these triggers lets you prepare and respond more effectively. For instance, if you know that last-minute requests stress you out, you could develop strategies for handling them more calmly, like prioritizing tasks or communicating your limits clearly.

Conclusion

Mastering the art of decoding your emotional toolkit is a vital first step towards harnessing the power of EQ for professional success. By understanding and managing both your own emotions and those of others, you can enhance your professional interactions, build stronger relationships, and contribute to a more effective and harmonious workplace.

As we move forward, remember that each skill you develop not only enriches your professional life but also deepens your personal growth and emotional well-being.

Emotional Regulation Self-Assessment

Instructions: Answer based on your typical reactions at work. Select the best option.

Questions:
1. **Reacting to Stress and Feedback:**
    A. React impulsively or take feedback personally.
    B. Pause or feel upset but listen.
    C. Analyze, control response, and use feedback constructively.
2. **Mindfulness and Handling Emotions:**
    A. Rarely practice mindfulness; emotions control actions.
    B. Occasionally practice; manage emotions with effort.
    C. Regularly practice; consciously manage emotions.
3. **Identifying and Managing Triggers:**
    A. Unsure of triggers; no strategy for negative emotions.
    B. Somewhat aware of triggers; use logic to calm down.
    C. Fully aware; use techniques like deep breathing.
4. **Preparation for Emotional Situations:**
    A. Focus only on content.
    B. Mentally prepare for feelings.
    C. Use strategies like visualization and positive self-talk.

Scoring:
- **Mostly A's:** Enhance emotional regulation strategies.
- **Mostly B's:** Good awareness; increase consistency in practice.
- **Mostly C's:** Excellent skills; potential for mentoring others.

Reflection: Evaluate your answers to pinpoint areas for improvement. Effective emotional regulation enhances both professional and personal well-being.

CALL TO ACTION
Implementing Your Emotional Toolkit

Now that you've explored the fundamentals of decoding your emotional toolkit, take a moment today to practice emotional journaling.

Reflect on a recent workday and write down a few key emotions you experienced, what triggered them, and how they influenced your interactions or decisions.

This simple practice will enhance your self-awareness and set the foundation for effective emotional management in your professional life.

2 STRATEGIES FOR EMOTIONAL REGULATION

Chapter 2: Strategies for Emotional Regulation

Welcome to the chapter that could change how you handle every challenging situation at work. Emotional regulation isn't just about keeping your cool. It's about understanding, managing, and directing your emotions to work in your favor—helping you make better decisions, maintain strong relationships, and advance your career.

Name the emotion	Validate the emotion	Identify triggers
Mediation or mindfullness	Talking through emotions	Journalling
Notice when you need a breakk	Good sleep hygiene	Consider therapy

Why Emotional Regulation Matters

Emotional regulation is crucial for professional growth and effectiveness. It involves more than suppressing negative feelings; it's about consciously transforming your emotional responses to promote a positive work environment and achieve your professional goals.

Imagine you're facing a tight deadline or a critical feedback session. How you manage your response to these situations can significantly impact your productivity, relationships, and overall career trajectory. Emotional regulation allows you to approach these scenarios with a level head and a strategy, rather than reacting impulsively.

Core Techniques for Mastering Emotional Regulation

To truly benefit from emotional regulation, you need practical strategies that can be applied daily. Here's how you can start:

- **Self-Awareness Exercises:** Begin by identifying your emotional triggers. What situations at work make you feel anxious, frustrated, or defensive? Regular self-reflection through journaling or mindfulness practices can help you recognize these triggers and prepare you to handle them better.
- **Cognitive Reappraisal:** This powerful technique involves changing your thought patterns about a particular situation to alter your emotional response. For instance, instead of viewing a challenging project as a potential failure point, see it as an opportunity to showcase your skills and learn new ones. This shift in perspective can reduce anxiety and increase motivation.
- **Emotional De-escalation:** When emotions flare, de-escalation techniques like deep breathing, brief meditation, or even a quick walk can help reduce their intensity, allowing you to think more clearly and respond more effectively.

> **A NIGHT IN THE EMERGENCY ROOM**
>
> Dr. Eman, an emergency room physician in a busy hospital in Bahrain, faced one of her most challenging shifts during a particularly harsh summer night. An influx of patients, ranging from minor injuries to severe traumas, put the team under immense pressure. Amidst this chaos, Dr. Eman received news that a patient she had grown particularly close to during previous shifts had passed away. This news was a heavy emotional blow in an already taxing situation.
>
> Despite her grief and the high emotional stakes, Dr. Eman knew that her ability to regulate her emotions was crucial not only for her performance but also for her team's morale. She took a brief moment to herself, practiced deep breathing exercises, and used cognitive reappraisal, reminding herself of the importance of her role and the immediate needs of her patients. By reframing her thoughts from feelings of loss to a focus on the lives she could still impact, Dr. Eman managed to navigate the rest of her shift with compassion and efficiency.
>
> Her emotional regulation that night not only helped her cope but also set a strong example for her team, demonstrating leadership and resilience under pressure.

Applying Emotions Constructively

Emotions can be a powerful motivator when harnessed correctly. Here's how you can channel them constructively:

- **Leveraging Emotional Energy:** The energy behind strong emotions like passion or anger can be redirected towards positive outcomes. For example, if you're upset about a missed opportunity, use that energy to propel yourself towards finding new opportunities or solutions.
- **Developing Emotional Agility:** Being emotionally agile means being able to adjust your emotional responses to better suit different situations. This is especially useful in leadership, where the ability to read and adapt to the

emotional needs of your team can enhance performance and morale.

Real-Life Success Stories

Consider the story of Layla, a project manager who used emotional regulation strategies to steer her team through a high-stakes project. By practicing mindfulness and cognitive reappraisal, she maintained her composure and inspired her team to overcome anxiety and deliver their best work under pressure.

Conclusion: Emotional Regulation as a Career Tool

By mastering the strategies outlined in this chapter, you will not only improve your personal well-being but also become a more effective and respected professional. Emotional regulation is key to navigating the complexities of modern work environments with confidence and tact.

As we progress through this book, remember that each technique you learn is a step towards becoming a more emotionally intelligent professional, equipped to tackle any challenge with grace and strategic insight.

CALL TO ACTION
Implement Emotional Regulation Today

Reflect on today's workday and identify a moment when you felt a strong emotion, whether positive or negative.

Apply the cognitive reappraisal technique: rethink the situation to view it from a different perspective, focusing on the learning opportunities it presented rather than just the emotional impact.

Write down this reflection and how changing your perspective altered your emotional response.

Aim to use this technique daily to gradually enhance your emotional regulation skills, leading to better decisions and stronger relationships at work.

3 ENHANCING COMMUNICATION WITH EQ

Chapter 3: Enhancing Communication with EQ

Unlocking the Power of Emotionally Intelligent Communication

Effective communication transcends mere information exchange; it involves making your message resonate, adapting to diverse audiences, and advancing enduring understanding and relationships. This chapter delves into how integrating emotional intelligence (EQ) into your communication strategies can profoundly improve your effectiveness in the workplace.

The Essence of EQ in Communication

Emotionally intelligent communication requires understanding your own feelings and those of others. This approach enhances clarity, ensures alignment of intentions with the emotional context of interactions, and builds trust and rapport.

Empathy: The Heartbeat of Effective Communication

The ability to understand and share others' feelings, is the foundation of effective communication. It enhances connections by making interactions more genuine and impactful.

Key Strategies for Empathetic Communication:

- **Active Listening:** Fully engage with the speaker, understand the nuances of their message, and respond thoughtfully to show respect and mutual understanding.
- **Mindful Speaking:** Be conscious of your tone and the words you choose, aiming to communicate clearly and compassionately.
- **Non-Verbal Cues:** Pay close attention to body language, both yours and that of others, as non-verbal signals often reveal more about feelings than words.

TRANSFORMING CLIENT RELATIONSHIPS THROUGH EQ

Context: This story is about a consultant named Mohammed, who specializes in crisis management and operates in a high-stakes, fast-paced consulting environment. Mohammed often deals with clients who are experiencing significant business disruptions, which means emotions can run high.

Story: Mohammed once worked with a client in the financial sector who was facing a severe data breach, leading to potential financial loss and reputational damage. The client's team was visibly stressed and defensive, which initially made communications tense and unproductive.

Mohammed realized that addressing the emotional climate was as crucial as solving the data breach itself. He began by acknowledging the stress and anxiety that the client's team felt, expressing genuine concern and understanding for their situation.

This empathetic approach helped to lower defenses, allowing for more open and effective communication. Mohammed then facilitated a meeting where he encouraged each team member to express their concerns and fears. He listened actively, responding with empathy and validating their emotions, which helped the team feel heard and supported.

As trust developed, Mohammed was able to guide the team more effectively through the crisis management process. His ability to manage emotions and communicate empathetically under pressure led to a successful resolution of the crisis.

The client credited Mohammed not only for his technical expertise but also for his emotional intelligence, which kept the team cohesive and focused during a critical time.

Outcome: The experience transformed how the client's company approached crisis management, leading them to prioritize EQ training for their leaders to improve how they manage teams and client relationships in high-pressure situations.

Navigating Conflicts with Emotional Savvy

Handling conflicts is a natural aspect of professional environments. Using EQ to manage these disagreements transforms potential confrontations into opportunities for personal and collective growth.

Effective Conflict Resolution Techniques:

- **Seek to Understand Before Being Understood:** By first understanding the other's perspective, you minimize defensiveness and adopt a dialogue based on respect and mutual understanding.
- **Focus on the Issue, Not the Person:** Maintain a professional tone and keep the discussion centered on resolving the issue, which preserves relationships and promotes constructive outcomes.
- **Manage Your Emotional Responses:** Recognize when your emotions are intensifying and take steps to calm down, which can prevent the situation from escalating and help you think more clearly.

Real-World Applications of EQ in Communication

Consider the following examples that illustrate the power of EQ in enhancing workplace communication:

- **Layla, a Marketing Director:** By using empathetic communication, she was able to uncover the root causes of her team's low morale and address them effectively, significantly improving productivity.
- **Khalid, a Construction Manager:** His proactive use of EQ during project delays enabled him to manage team conflicts efficiently, keeping the project on track.

Mastering Communication with EQ

By employing the strategies outlined in this chapter, you will enhance your ability to handle daily interactions and challenging conversations more effectively, build stronger relationships, and promote a supportive and productive work environment.

Conclusion

This chapter has provided you with the essential tools to enhance your professional interactions through emotionally intelligent communication. As you continue to integrate these practices, you will not only see improvements in your professional relationships but also in your overall career success.

Reflective Journal Prompt:

Reflect on a recent communication challenge at work by considering the following questions:

- **Describe the Situation:** What was the nature of the communication challenge? Who was involved, and what were the stakes?
- **Identify Your Emotions:** What emotions did you feel during the interaction? Were these emotions helpful or hindering?
- **Analyze Your Approach:** How did your emotional state influence your communication style? Were you able to apply empathy effectively?
- **Evaluate the Outcomes:** How did the interaction conclude? What was the impact of your communication approach on the outcome?
- **Consider Alternative Approaches:** Reflecting on the principles of EQ discussed in this chapter, what could you have done differently to enhance the communication outcome?
- **Plan for Future Interactions:** Based on this reflection, how can you adjust your communication strategy in future similar situations to apply EQ more effectively?

This reflective exercise is designed to help you critically apply the lessons from this chapter to your own experiences, deepening your understanding and enhancing your skills in EQ-based communication.

CALL TO ACTION
Apply Your Learning

As you close this chapter on enhancing communication with EQ, challenge yourself to put these concepts into action.

Over the next week, focus on employing active listening in all your professional interactions.

Make a conscious effort to fully engage with your colleagues, paying close attention to both their words and the emotions behind them.

Reflect on how this practice impacts your communication effectiveness and relationships at work.

4 CULTIVATING EMOTIONAL RESILIENCE

Chapter 4: Cultivating Emotional Resilience

In the fast-paced and often high-pressure environment of modern workplaces, where challenges like tight deadlines, performance expectations, and complex team dynamics are common, developing emotional resilience becomes a key skill for anyone looking to thrive. This chapter explores how you can build and maintain resilience—an ability that allows you to navigate the ups and downs of your career with grace and determination.

Understanding Emotional Resilience

Emotional resilience is the capacity to recover quickly from difficulties, adapt to change, and keep going in the face of adversity. It's about bouncing back from setbacks and using experiences as stepping-stones to success. Resilient professionals don't just survive tough situations; they find ways to grow because of them.

Components of Emotional Resilience

- **Self-Awareness:** Knowing what you feel and why you feel it is the first step toward resilience. It's about being aware of your emotional triggers and understanding how they impact your thoughts and actions.
- **Self-Regulation:** This is your ability to control your emotional reactions. It means not just reacting on impulse but choosing how to respond in a way that aligns with your goals and values.
- **Optimism:** Maintaining a hopeful outlook on life makes a big difference. It's about seeing the glass as half full, believing in your abilities, and expecting good things to happen.
- **Problem-Solving:** Being able to find solutions to problems under pressure is a crucial part of being resilient. It involves staying calm and thinking clearly when things get tough.
- **Support Networks:** No one achieves anything alone. Having a strong network of colleagues, friends, and family can provide you with the backing you need to overcome work challenges.

After exploring the foundational concepts of emotional resilience, let's look at a real-life example from the healthcare sector, where high stakes and high stress are part of the daily environment. Sameera's story demonstrates how emotional resilience is not just theoretical but a practical, vital skill in navigating both professional challenges and personal well-being.

> **OVERCOMING ADVERSITY IN EMERGENCY HEALTHCARE**
>
> **Background:** Sameera, an emergency room (ER) nurse in a busy hospital in Riyadh, faces high-pressure situations daily. Her ability to maintain emotional resilience not only supports her mental health but also ensures she can provide the best care to patients in critical conditions.

> **Story:** During a particularly intense night shift, Sameera encountered a surge of patients resulting from a major accident. The overwhelming influx tested her limits as she navigated through critical decisions and life-saving actions. Despite the chaos, Sameera utilized her emotional resilience training to manage her stress and maintain a calm demeanor. She focused on her breathing, used positive self-talk, and leveraged her support network, including colleagues who understood the emotional toll of their work.
>
> One moment stood out when a young patient, visibly scared and in pain, was brought in. Recognizing the fear in the child's eyes, Sameera took a moment to compose herself, ensuring her own emotions were in check before she approached. She then used a calm, reassuring tone, explaining the procedures in a way that comforted the child, effectively managing her professional responsibilities while also addressing the emotional needs of her patient.
>
> **Impact:** This incident not only highlighted Sameera's ability to manage her own emotional state under pressure but also reflected her impact on others' emotional well-being. Her resilience ensured that she remained an effective caregiver during a crisis, demonstrating leadership and empathy in a high-stress environment.

Building Resilience Through Everyday Practices

How can you build these skills? Here are some everyday practices that can help:

- **Mindfulness and Meditation:** Regular practice can enhance your self-awareness and help you manage stress better.
- **Reflective Journaling:** Writing about your day and how you felt can give you insights into your emotional patterns and triggers.
- **Setting and Achieving Small Goals:** This builds confidence and reinforces your ability to manage challenges.
- **Seeking Feedback:** Open yourself to constructive criticism and use it to strengthen your problem-solving skills.

Real-Life Applications of Emotional Resilience

Let's look at how emotional resilience plays out in the real world:

- **A Project Manager's Challenge:** Imagine a project manager facing unexpected setbacks. By applying resilience strategies such as seeking support and using problem-solving skills, they can navigate the project back on track.
- **Handling High-Pressure Negotiations:** A sales professional using deep breathing techniques to stay calm during a tough negotiation demonstrates resilience by managing stress in real-time.

Creating a Resilient Workplace

Organizations play a crucial role in encouraging resilience among their employees. Here are a few ways companies can build a more resilient workforce:

- **Resilience Training:** Workshops on stress management, mindfulness, and emotional intelligence can be part of regular training.
- **Supportive Culture:** Encouraging open dialogue about challenges and failures makes it easier for employees to seek help and feedback without fear.
- **Recognition and Rewards:** Acknowledging employees' efforts to overcome challenges can reinforce resilient behaviors across the organization.

Conclusion: Thriving Through Resilience

This chapter has shown you how to cultivate the kind of emotional resilience that will not only help you deal with the challenges of today's workplace but also turn them into opportunities for personal and professional growth. As you continue to develop your resilience, you'll find that you're not just surviving; you're thriving, able to face up to whatever your professional life throws at you with confidence and poise.

Embrace these practices, and watch as they transform your approach to challenges, enhance your career, and enrich your overall life experience.

CALL TO ACTION
Start Building Your Resilience Today

This week, select one of the resilience-building practices discussed in this chapter and integrate it into your daily routine.

You might choose to start a reflective journal, practice mindfulness for a few minutes each day, or set and achieve a small, manageable goal.

Track how this practice impacts your emotional resilience at work and in your personal life.

At the end of the week, reflect on the changes you've noticed: Are you feeling more capable of handling stress? Do you recover from setbacks more quickly?

Use your observations to refine your approach and choose another practice to implement in the following week.

Keep this cycle of practice and reflection going to strengthen your resilience continuously.

5 EQ FOR LEADERSHIP

Chapter 5: EQ for Leadership

Introduction to Emotional Leadership

In today's complex business environment, the essence of leadership has evolved beyond traditional command-and-control models to include a more empathetic and emotionally aware approach. This chapter explores emotional leadership, a nuanced form of leadership that utilizes emotional intelligence (EQ) to inspire, empower, and guide individuals and teams towards achieving their highest potential.

Head-Based Attributes	Heart-Based Attributes
• Curiosity • Wisdom • Perspective • Capability	• Humility • Self-awareness • Courage • Empathy

Understanding Emotional Leadership

Emotional leadership is about influencing and guiding teams not just through logical decision-making but through the empathetic and mindful engagement of each team member's strengths and emotions. It involves understanding and managing both one's own emotions and those of others to nurture a supportive and productive work environment.

Core Principles of Emotional Leadership

1. **Self-awareness:** Leaders must have a deep understanding of their own emotional triggers and how they affect their behavior and decisions.
2. **Self-regulation:** This involves managing one's emotions to stay calm and clear-headed, even in crisis situations.

3. **Motivation:** Using emotional drivers to pursue goals with energy and persistence is essential for maintaining team morale and focus.
4. **Empathy:** The ability to understand and share the feelings of others, which is crucial for managing teams compassionately and effectively.
5. **Social skills:** These are needed to manage and build relationships, resolve conflicts, and inspire and lead others effectively.

The Role of Empathy in Leadership

Empathy is at the heart of emotional leadership. It enables leaders to connect with their teams on a personal level, enhancing mutual respect and understanding. Empathetic leaders are adept at recognizing the emotional needs of their team members and addressing them in a way that encourages productivity and loyalty.

> **TRANSFORMATION THROUGH EMOTIONAL LEADERSHIP**
>
> As an illustration of emotional leadership in action, consider the story of Ali, a regional manager at a large healthcare organization in Oman. Ali faced a significant challenge during the peak of the COVID-19 pandemic. Tasked with leading his team through a period of extreme uncertainty and stress, he realized that traditional management techniques were not sufficient. He needed to connect with his team on a deeper emotional level to keep morale high and maintain productivity.
>
> Recognizing the fear and anxiety among his team members, Ali began holding weekly virtual meetings dedicated solely to addressing team members' concerns, listening to their personal challenges, and offering support. He used these sessions not only to provide updates but to openly share his own feelings about the crisis, which helped to create an atmosphere of mutual trust and vulnerability.
>
> This empathetic approach allowed Ali to understand the specific needs of his team better, adapt workloads accordingly, and

> implement flexible schedules to accommodate their personal circumstances. His ability to empathize and respond with emotional intelligence led to increased team cohesion and resilience, maintaining high patient care standards despite the crisis.
>
> The impact of his leadership style extended beyond immediate crisis management. His team emerged stronger, with a renewed sense of loyalty and commitment to the organization, illustrating the lasting benefits of emotionally intelligent leadership.
>
> This example highlights the profound influence that emotional intelligence can have in leadership roles, particularly during times of crisis. It underscores the importance of empathy, understanding, and genuine emotional connection in guiding teams through challenging circumstances.

Developing Emotional Leadership

Developing strong emotional leadership skills involves continuous learning and practice. Here are some strategies to enhance your emotional leadership capabilities:

- **Active Listening:** Engage fully with team members, listening to understand their perspectives and concerns without prematurely judging or responding.
- **Regular Feedback:** Provide clear, constructive feedback in a supportive manner. Focus on the behavior, not the person, to improve improvement and learning.
- **Conflict Resolution:** Address conflicts openly and patiently, focusing on the issue at hand rather than personal grievances.
- **Inspiring Others:** Share a compelling vision that motivates and aligns team efforts. Recognize and celebrate achievements that contribute to this vision.

Expanding Influence Through Emotional Leadership

Leaders who effectively manage their emotions and those of their teams can significantly influence their organization's culture and productivity. They create environments where problems are solved through collaboration and innovation, and where team members feel valued and understood.

Conclusion: The Future of Leadership

Emotional leadership is crucial for navigating the complexities of modern organizational life. As you continue to enhance your EQ skills, you'll not only become a more effective leader but also contribute to a more emotionally intelligent, responsive, and successful organization.

Reflective Journal Prompt

As part of your development as an emotional leader, maintain a reflective journal.

Use the following prompt after encountering leadership challenges to deepen your understanding and improve your approach:

- **Leadership Situation:** Describe a recent situation where you needed to lead your team through a challenge. Detail the context and your role in the scenario.
- **Emotional Response:** What emotions did you experience during this situation? How did these feelings influence your actions?
- **Impact on Team Dynamics:** Reflect on how your emotional response affected the team's dynamics. Did it enhance cohesion, trust, and productivity, or did it create tension and confusion?
- **Lessons Learned and Future Strategies:** What did you learn from this experience about your strengths and areas needing improvement in emotional leadership? Outline strategies you plan to implement in future leadership scenarios to enhance your effectiveness.

CALL TO ACTION
Implementing Emotional Leadership

Reflect on today's interactions with your team or colleagues and identify one moment where emotional leadership could have improved the outcome.

Tomorrow, focus on applying the principle of empathy in your communications—actively listen to understand feelings and perspectives, and respond thoughtfully.

This practice will help you connect on a deeper level and enhance team dynamics.

Note any changes in response or atmosphere and use these observations to refine your leadership approach continuously.

6 EQ IN TEAM DYNAMICS

Chapter 6: EQ in Team Dynamics

Introduction to Emotional Intelligence in Teams

In this chapter, where we delve into the pivotal role of emotional intelligence (EQ) in creating effective and harmonious teams. In any professional setting, the success of projects often depends on the ability of teams to work cohesively. This chapter explores how EQ not only strengthens team interactions but also enhances overall team performance. We will discuss why EQ is crucial in team settings, provide strategies for promoting team EQ, and share inspiring stories from real teams who've transformed their dynamics through emotional intelligence.

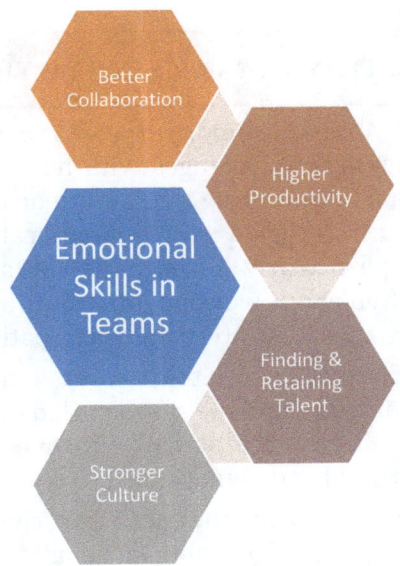

Why Team EQ Matters

Successful teamwork goes beyond individual competence; it requires a synergy that can only be achieved when team members understand and manage both their emotions and those of others. High team EQ results in improved communication, stronger interpersonal relationships, and a robust capacity to face challenges together. Teams that operate with high EQ are marked by a deep sense of trust and a shared commitment to goals, making them more adaptable and effective.

Understanding and Managing Team Emotions

The foundation of team EQ lies in understanding the emotional currents within the team. Emotional awareness involves recognizing how each team member's feelings affect their behavior and the team's overall dynamics. For example, a team leader might notice a member consistently withdrawing during discussions about tight deadlines. By addressing this sensitively, the leader can help the member manage their anxiety, thereby improving their engagement and the team's productivity.

TRANSFORMING TEAM DYNAMICS IN HEALTHCARE

Background: Dr. Amina, a senior surgeon at a major hospital in Kuwait, faced significant challenges with her multi-disciplinary team. The team, consisting of surgeons, nurses, and administrative staff, struggled with communication breakdowns and high stress, particularly during long shifts. Disagreements were common, often about workload distributions and decision-making processes, which negatively affected patient care.

Situation: During a particularly tense week, a misunderstanding between the nursing staff and the surgeons led to a surgical delay, which not only impacted the patient outcome but also left the team feeling frustrated and demoralized.

EQ Intervention: Realizing the need for change, Dr. Amina decided to employ her EQ skills to rebuild team trust and communication. She initiated a series of team meetings where each member was encouraged to express their concerns and emotions without judgment. Dr. Amina focused on actively listening and empathizing with her team, acknowledging the emotional toll of their roles, and the pressures they faced.

Outcome: These meetings opened up new lines of communication and understanding. Dr. Amina used the insights gained to implement a new protocol that included structured

> debriefs after each surgery and a rotating leadership role within the team to distribute decision-making power. Over time, these changes led to improved morale, a smoother workflow, and better patient outcomes.
>
> **Reflection**: Dr. Amina reflected on this experience in a departmental newsletter, emphasizing how a focus on emotional intelligence—particularly empathy and active listening—was crucial in transforming team dynamics. She noted that recognizing and validating the team's emotions helped in promoting a sense of community and mutual respect, which was instrumental in overcoming operational challenges.

Enhancing Emotional Dynamics

Effective team leaders use EQ to navigate and harmonize the diverse emotional landscapes of their team members. This involves not only recognizing but also respecting and valuing the varied emotional expressions within the team. It also includes:

1. **Promoting Emotional Expression**: Encourage an environment where team members feel safe to express their feelings and perspectives. This could involve regular emotional check-ins or dedicated time during meetings for team members to share their thoughts and feelings.
2. **Developing Collective Emotional Strategies**: Train teams in emotional regulation techniques such as mindfulness or stress reduction exercises. These skills help teams handle high-pressure situations more calmly and cohesively.

Building Emotional Cohesion

Cultivating emotional cohesion within a team enhances its stability and performance. This involves adopting a supportive and empathetic team culture where emotional openness and mutual support are norms. Techniques include:

1. **Team-building Activities**: Regular, structured activities designed to enhance interpersonal relations and build trust.
2. **Conflict Resolution Training**: Equip teams with the skills to handle disagreements constructively, ensuring conflicts are resolved in ways that strengthen team bonds rather than weaken them.

Case Studies: EQ Transforming Teams

- **Tech Team Turnaround**: A software development team in Dubai was experiencing conflict and low morale due to miscommunication and high stress. After a series of EQ workshops focusing on communication and empathy, team members learned to express their concerns and listen to others effectively. This led to improved morale and a noticeable increase in productivity.
- **Hospitality Team Success**: At a hotel in Manama, the guest services team struggled with high turnover and poor customer feedback. Training in EQ, particularly in understanding and managing emotions, helped the team develop stronger rapport with guests and each other, resulting in improved service ratings and reduced staff turnover.

Practical Tools and Techniques for Teams

To advance and maintain high EQ within teams, consider implementing the following tools:

1. **Emotional Awareness Tools**: Such as mood meters or emotion diaries that help team members articulate and track their feelings.
2. **Stress Management Workshops**: Focus on techniques like deep breathing exercises, guided meditations, or progressive muscle relaxation, which can be practiced during breaks or before starting a stressful task.

3. **Regular EQ Assessments**: Use tools like the Emotional Competence Inventory to measure and monitor the team's emotional skills and progress.

Conclusion

Emotional intelligence is essential for the success of teams in today's collaborative work environments. This chapter has outlined how EQ can be strategically developed within teams to enhance their functionality, resilience, and productivity. By investing in EQ, teams not only improve their work output but also their workplace satisfaction and overall well-being.

Interactive Scenarios (Role-Play Simulations): EQ in Team Dynamics

Overview: Manage a diverse project team in Bahrain, addressing tensions and communication barriers.

Objective: Enhance team communication and resolve conflicts using EQ.

Roles:
- Project Manager
- Team Members from Bahrain, Saudi Arabia, Kuwait, and Qatar

Scenario: Address challenges during a team meeting where interpersonal conflicts and frustration are evident.

Tasks:
1. Identify emotional cues and triggers.
2. Engage in empathetic communication.
3. Facilitate strategies for better communication and cohesion.
4. Encourage open emotional expression.

Interactive Elements:
- Choose responses showcasing EQ.
- Get feedback on decisions.
- Reflect on the impact and potential improvements.

Outcomes:
- Improved communication and understanding.
- Stronger team cohesion.
- Enhanced productivity by overcoming cultural barriers.

Reflection Questions:
- Insights on team emotions?
- Impact of your choices on dynamics?
- Adjustments for real-world application?

CALL TO ACTION
Emotional Awareness in Your Team

This week, take the initiative to enhance emotional awareness within your team.

Organize a brief, informal meeting where each team member shares one emotional insight about themselves—something that affects their work life, like a common stressor or a motivational factor.

Use this opportunity to practice active listening and encourage a supportive dialogue among team members.

This exercise will not only strengthen your team's emotional cohesion but also provide valuable insights that can help you manage team dynamics more effectively.

Remember, the goal is to create an environment where emotional transparency becomes a bridge to greater teamwork and success.

7 ETHICAL LEADERSHIP AND DECISION-MAKING WITH EQ

Chapter 7: Ethical Leadership and Decision-Making with EQ

Why Ethical Leadership Matters

In a world where headlines often reveal scandals and ethical missteps, ethical leadership stands as a beacon of integrity and trust. This chapter delves into how emotional intelligence (EQ) can forge leaders who are not only successful but also principled and respected. Ethical leaders wield their influence to champion fairness, honesty, and integrity, setting a standard that permeates their entire organizations.

Ethical leadership is more than making morally sound decisions; it's about leading in a way that promotes a positive, ethical culture that influences everyone from top executives to entry-level employees. This type of leadership enhances company reputation, cultivates trust, and drives sustainable success.

The Role of EQ in Ethical Leadership

Emotional intelligence is indispensable for ethical leadership. It empowers leaders to understand and empathize with others, foresee the outcomes of their decisions, and manage the emotional dynamics that ethical decisions often stir. Leaders with high EQ are adept at navigating the complex moral landscapes of modern organizations, making decisions that are not only good for business but also good for the broader community.

Core Aspects of Ethical Leadership with EQ

- **Empathy and Awareness:** A leader's ability to genuinely understand and share the feelings of others ensures that decisions are made with a comprehensive view of their impacts on all stakeholders.
- **Self-Regulation:** Leaders must manage their emotions to uphold their ethical standards consistently, especially in challenging situations.
- **Moral Reasoning:** EQ enhances a leader's capacity to weigh various ethical considerations, integrating emotional insights with rational analysis to arrive at decisions that align with both organizational values and social norms.

Developing Ethical Leaders through EQ

Building ethical leaders requires a focused approach to developing specific EQ competencies:

- **Training in Empathy:** Workshops and training sessions that improve leaders' ability to understand and share the emotions of others, enhancing their sensitivity to ethical dilemmas.
- **Cultivating Self-awareness:** Programs designed to help leaders recognize their values, biases, and the emotional drivers of their decision-making processes.

- **Strengthening Emotional Courage:** Encouraging leaders to take principled stands, even when they face pressure to do otherwise.

Practical Applications of EQ in Ethical Decision-Making

To illustrate how EQ can be applied in ethical leadership, consider the following scenarios:

- **Scenario 1:** A leader discovers financial discrepancies in their department. Instead of covering them up to meet short-term targets, the leader uses EQ to assess the potential long-term impacts on stakeholder trust and decides to report the issue transparently, leading to corrective actions and enhanced team training to prevent future issues.
- **Scenario 2:** During downsizing, a leader uses their EQ skills to handle the process with care and fairness, ensuring that decisions are communicated with empathy and support, helping the remaining employees adjust to the new situation and maintain morale.

Navigating the Gray Areas of Technology and Ethics. Let's consider a tangible example from the tech industry:

> **ETHICAL LEADERSHIP IN ACTION**
>
> Sarah, a CEO of a multinational tech company in Qatar, faced a significant ethical dilemma when she discovered that a profitable software project relied on data practices that, while legal, were widely considered unethical in terms of user privacy.
>
> Instead of pushing the issue under the rug to benefit from the lucrative deal, Sarah chose to reevaluate the project. She initiated a company-wide discussion about aligning business practices with core ethical values, leading to a reformed data policy that not only complied with higher ethical standards but also positioned the company as a leader in consumer privacy.

> This move initially caused a dip in the company's stock price but earned widespread praise from industry experts and customers, eventually leading to long-term gains in both reputation and financial performance.

Sarah's story provides a clear illustration of how emotional intelligence can guide ethical leadership. By choosing to prioritize ethical standards over immediate profits, she not only safeguarded her company's integrity but also boosted its long-term success. Her decision required understanding the emotional impacts on all stakeholders, showcasing the powerful role of EQ in navigating ethical complexities.

Incorporating EQ into Organizational Ethics Programs

Integrating EQ into an organization's ethical framework involves several strategic actions:

- **Ethics Audits:** Regular evaluations of company practices and policies through an EQ lens to ensure they adopt an ethical and emotionally intelligent work environment.
- **Stakeholder Feedback:** Using EQ to interpret and act on feedback from employees, customers, and the community, ensuring that the organization's practices align with broader ethical standards.
- **Leadership Development:** Creating pathways for emerging leaders to develop high EQ, preparing them to uphold and propagate ethical standards.

Challenges and Opportunities

While integrating EQ and ethics presents challenges, such as navigating complex emotional and ethical landscapes, it also offers significant opportunities to redefine leadership success. Ethical leaders can transform their workplaces, inspire their teams, and drive change that aligns with societal values.

Conclusion: The Ethical Path Forward

As we close this chapter, we emphasize that ethical leadership fortified by emotional intelligence is not merely a legal or compliance requirement but a foundational element of modern organizational success. Leaders who embrace EQ and ethics position themselves and their organizations for enduring success and respect in the global marketplace.

Interactive Scenario: Ethical Leadership in Practice

Overview: Role-play as a Regional Manager in Bahrain, tackling a corruption case while balancing emotional and ethical decision-making.

Background: Uncover discrepancies in contracts suggesting senior manager kickbacks. Address these issues considering their impact on team morale and organizational ethics.

Objectives:
- Evaluate emotional and ethical dimensions.
- Navigate stakeholder meetings to inform and resolve issues.
- Maintain organizational trust and integrity.

Role-Play Steps:
1. **Initial Review:** Examine case details and assess team emotions.
2. **Stakeholder Meetings:** Engage with the accused manager, team, and HR/legal departments using empathy and strategic communication.
3. **Decision Making:** Analyze information and emotional insights to determine the next steps, from investigations to disciplinary actions.
4. **Feedback and Reflection:** Receive feedback and reflect on your emotional management and ethical choices.

Outcome: Evaluate your capability in ethical leadership and emotional intelligence, with feedback on key skills and areas for improvement.

CALL TO ACTION
Practice Ethical Leadership

This week, identify a decision-making moment in your work where ethical considerations are prominent.

Reflect on the ethical implications and the emotions involved.

Engage in a discussion with a key stakeholder to empathetically understand their perspective and feelings about the situation.

Make a decision that aligns with your organization's ethical standards and enhances emotional well-being.

At the week's end, review the outcome and your emotional management.

Consider how EQ influenced the decision and identify areas for improvement.

This practice not only reinforces ethical leadership but also enhances your emotional intelligence in professional settings.

8 THE FUTURE OF EQ IN PROFESSIONAL DEVELOPMENT

Chapter 8: The Future of EQ in Professional Development

In this chapter, we'll explore the horizon of emotional intelligence (EQ) in the evolving landscape of professional development. As we advance further into the 21st century, the dynamics of the workplace are transforming at an unprecedented pace, influenced by technological advancements, globalization, and changing organizational structures. In this environment, EQ emerges not just as a beneficial skill but as a critical element for professional success and adaptation.

EQ in a Technologically Advanced World

In today's digital era, where artificial intelligence and automation are becoming the norm, the unique capabilities that EQ offers—such as empathy, understanding, and emotional management—are increasingly vital. These skills enable professionals to excel in roles that technology cannot fulfill, particularly in leadership, customer relations, and team dynamics. As machines take on more cognitive tasks, it's the emotional intelligence of human professionals that will dictate the quality of interactions and the depth of customer engagement.

Globalization and Cultural Intelligence

As businesses expand globally, professionals encounter diverse work cultures and practices. EQ becomes indispensable in navigating these complexities. It allows individuals to bridge cultural divides, manage diverse teams effectively, and encourage inclusive workplaces. This chapter discusses how enhancing one's EQ can lead to better understanding and cooperation among team members from various cultural backgrounds, thereby enhancing overall organizational effectiveness.

The Rise of Remote Work

The recent surge in remote work has brought new challenges in team management and communication. Emotional intelligence is critical in this context, as it helps leaders and team members to adopt connections and maintain engagement without face-to-face interactions. EQ skills enable individuals to pick up on subtle cues in virtual meetings or written communications, ensuring that the team remains aligned and motivated, despite physical distance.

In the rapidly evolving workplace, remote work has become more than just a trend—it's a mainstay. This shift demands new competencies, especially in emotional intelligence. In remote work environments, the absence of physical presence and reduced non-verbal cues challenge even the most experienced professionals. Emotional intelligence becomes the key to bridging these gaps. It allows managers and team members alike to enhance connection, anticipate the needs of others, and communicate effectively despite physical distances.

> **EMBRACING EQ IN A REMOTE WORK ENVIRONMENT**
>
> Jamal, a project manager for a tech startup based in Jeddah, navigates a fully remote team spanning across Saudi and the rest of GCC. With the sudden shift to remote work due to health safety concerns, Jamal faced significant challenges in keeping his team motivated and cohesive. Using his EQ skills, he initiated virtual coffee breaks and regular one-on-one check-ins to gauge the team's morale. Over time, he noticed a marked improvement in communication and a decrease in misunderstandings and conflicts. His ability to empathize and actively listen helped him address issues before they escalated, keeping the team productive and engaged despite the physical distance.
>
> Quote from Jamal: "Emotional intelligence is our bridge when physical presence isn't possible. It allows us to understand and connect with each other deeply, even if we're only meeting through screens."

This example underscores the practical applications of emotional intelligence in maintaining team cohesion and productivity in remote settings. To develop these crucial EQ skills, professionals can engage in targeted exercises such as virtual role-playing sessions, which simulate challenging interactions and provide opportunities to practice empathy and active listening. Additionally, tools like digital emotion tracking apps can assist in monitoring and managing the emotional well-being of teams, facilitating a more supportive and connected remote work environment.

Further Application:

Implementing regular EQ training sessions that focus on remote communication and conflict resolution can also be incredibly beneficial. These initiatives not only enhance individual EQ competencies but also build a more resilient and adaptive organizational culture, well-equipped to thrive in the digital age.

Changing Work Environments and Team Dynamics

Modern workplaces often favor flexible, project-based teams over traditional, hierarchical structures. In such dynamic environments, EQ is essential for managing diverse team dynamics and ensuring collaborative success. This chapter provides insights into how EQ can be effectively used to manage emotions, resolve conflicts, and promote synergy within teams, leading to more innovative and effective project outcomes.

Continuous Development of EQ

Embracing EQ requires a commitment to lifelong learning. This section outlines various approaches for continuous EQ development, including formal education, self-directed learning, and experiential learning through coaching and feedback. We explore the benefits of each method and how professionals can integrate these into their personal development plans to continually enhance their EQ.

Strategies for Integrating EQ into Your Career

- **Formal Education and Certifications**: Many universities and professional training institutes now offer courses specifically designed to enhance EQ alongside technical skills, providing certifications that are highly valued in the job market.
- **Self-Directed Learning**: For those who prefer a self-paced approach, there are numerous books, online courses, and interactive tools that offer deep dives into various aspects of EQ.
- **Professional Workshops and Seminars**: Participating in workshops and seminars provides practical, hands-on experiences in EQ, facilitating real-time feedback and learning.
- **Coaching and Mentorship**: Engaging with a coach or mentor who specializes in emotional intelligence can

provide personalized insights and guidance, helping individuals to apply EQ principles in their specific professional contexts.

EQ for Leadership and Innovation

Leaders equipped with strong EQ are better able to inspire and motivate their teams, drive organizational change, and innovate business practices. This chapter highlights case studies where leaders have successfully applied EQ to transform their organizations, demonstrating the profound impact of emotionally intelligent leadership.

Building an EQ-Driven Culture

Organizations that prioritize EQ in their cultural framework see significant benefits, including higher employee engagement, reduced turnover, and stronger loyalty. We discuss strategies for embedding EQ into the organizational DNA, from recruitment and training to performance management and leadership development.

Looking to the Future: The Growing Demand for EQ

The demand for emotionally intelligent professionals is expected to increase as businesses recognize the value of human-centric skills in driving sustainable success.

Conclusion

As we conclude this exploration of the future of EQ in professional development, it's clear that emotional intelligence will play a pivotal role in shaping successful careers and innovative organizations. By investing in EQ now, professionals not only enhance their current capabilities but also prepare themselves for the challenges and opportunities of the future.

This chapter not only underscores the importance of developing EQ for professional growth but also provides actionable strategies for integrating EQ into your career development plan. As the professional landscape evolves, those equipped with strong EQ skills will lead the charge in navigating the complexities of modern workplaces.

CALL TO ACTION
Implement Your EQ Growth Plan

This week, take the first step towards integrating emotional intelligence into your professional development by identifying one EQ skill you wish to enhance.

Whether it's empathy, self-regulation, or effective communication, commit to a specific, measurable action.

Schedule a time each day to practice this skill, such as during team meetings, in your interactions with clients, or even in challenging situations.

Record your experiences and any changes you notice in interactions or your personal stress levels.

Share your progress with a mentor or peer to gain feedback and create accountability for your growth.

Let's make EQ a pivotal element of your career development starting today!

9 TOOLS AND RESOURCES FOR DEVELOPING EQ

Chapter 9: Tools & Resources for Enhancing EQ

This chapter is dedicated to equipping you with a diverse toolkit to enhance your emotional intelligence (EQ) through daily practices, structured workshops, and personal coaching. By engaging with these tools, you will transform your theoretical knowledge of EQ into tangible skills that can significantly benefit both your personal and professional life.

Understanding the Importance of Practical EQ Development

Developing your EQ goes beyond understanding emotions theoretically; it involves actively practicing and improving your emotional skills in real-life situations. In today's fast-paced work environments, particularly in culturally diverse regions like the Middle East, possessing a high EQ can set you apart as a competent leader, an effective team player, and a valued employee. It's essential for managing conflicts, navigating stressful situations, and enhancing interpersonal relations.

Daily Tools for Enhancing EQ

1. **Self-Assessment Tools**:
   - Begin by understanding your current level of emotional intelligence. Tools like the Emotional Intelligence Appraisal or the Mayer-Salovey-Caruso Emotional Intelligence Test (MSCEIT) provide a clear baseline measurement of your EQ strengths and areas that need improvement.
   - **Example**: Amir, a manager in Dubai, used these tools to discover he excelled in understanding others' emotions but needed to work on his own emotional regulation. This insight helped him tailor his EQ development efforts.
2. **EQ Apps**:
   - Mobile applications such as 'EQ Coach' or 'Mood Meter' offer convenient ways to practice EQ skills daily. These apps provide exercises, track emotional changes, and give feedback to help users manage their emotions effectively.
   - **Example**: Sarah, a consultant in Abu Dhabi, uses the 'EQ Coach' app to prepare for client meetings by setting emotional goals and reviewing performance afterward to ensure continuous improvement.
3. **Emotional Journals**:
   - Maintaining an emotional journal is an effective way to develop EQ by recording and reflecting on your emotional experiences and reactions. This practice helps identify patterns and triggers in your behavior.
   - **Example**: Layla, an HR professional in Riyadh, keeps a daily journal to track her emotional state at work, helping her manage stress and improve her decision-making under pressure.

Workshops and Training Programs

Before we delve into the specifics of how workshops and training programs can facilitate EQ development, let's consider the story of Ahmed, a software developer at a tech startup in Bahrain. His experience illustrates the transformative impact that EQ training can have on an individual's professional journey, particularly in high-pressure environments like those often found in the tech industry.

> **EMBRACING EQ IN TECH STARTUPS**
>
> Ahmed, a software developer at a rapidly growing tech startup in Bahrain, found himself overwhelmed by the pressure of his workload and the high expectations of his team. Despite his technical expertise, he struggled with managing stress and communicating effectively with his colleagues, which often led to misunderstandings and conflict. Realizing the need for a change,
>
> Ahmed attended an EQ development workshop recommended by his HR department. The training focused on emotional awareness and regulation techniques tailored for high-pressure environments.
>
> Over the next few months, Ahmed applied these techniques daily, notably using 'mindful pauses' before responding to emails and during meetings, which helped him maintain composure and think more clearly.
>
> The real turning point came during a critical project presentation. Instead of succumbing to his usual anxiety, Ahmed used visualization techniques he learned from the workshop to boost his confidence and deliver a clear and persuasive presentation. His improved emotional control not only impressed his team but also enhanced his ability to influence and lead within the project.
>
> Encouraged by his personal growth and the positive feedback from his peers, Ahmed became an advocate for integrating EQ training across the entire company, leading to a noticeable improvement in team dynamics and overall productivity.

1. **Customized EQ Workshops**:
    - Many organizations now offer workshops tailored to specific workplace needs, such as improving

leadership, enhancing team communication, or managing customer relations with emotional intelligence.
- o **Case Study**: A telecommunications company in Kuwait improved team cohesion and customer satisfaction scores dramatically after implementing EQ workshops that focused on empathetic communication and stress management.

2. **Online EQ Courses**:
   - o Comprehensive online platforms offer a variety of EQ courses that provide flexibility and depth. These courses, available on platforms like Coursera, Udemy, and LinkedIn Learning, cover topics from basic emotional awareness to advanced applications in leadership.
   - o **Example**: Hameed, an IT manager in Doha, enhanced his team management skills by completing a series of online courses focused on emotional intelligence in leadership.

One-on-One EQ Coaching

- For personalized development, EQ coaching offers tailored guidance. Certified EQ coaches help individuals explore their emotional patterns, set specific improvement goals, and provide strategies and feedback.
- **Case Study**: Mona, a finance director in Manama, engaged an EQ coach to improve her leadership during a company merger. The coaching focused on strategic emotional management, aiding her in maintaining team morale and engagement through the transition.

Implementing EQ in Professional Settings

- **Daily EQ Challenges**:
    - Implement small, daily challenges that focus on practicing specific EQ skills, such as active listening or expressing empathy.
    - **Example**: Tariq, a sales leader in Muscat, sets daily challenges for his team to practice specific EQ skills during client interactions, which has led to increased sales and improved client feedback.
- **Structured Reflection**:
    - Encourage regular reflection on interactions and situations where EQ was or could have been effectively applied. This can lead to better emotional habits and more thoughtful responses in future interactions.
    - **Example**: Aisha, a project coordinator in Dubai, uses structured reflection during weekly team meetings to discuss where EQ was successfully employed and where opportunities were missed.

Conclusion

This chapter arms you with a robust set of tools and strategies designed to advance your emotional intelligence development. By incorporating these resources into your daily routines and professional practices, you will see a profound transformation in how you understand and interact with the world around you. As you continue to develop your EQ, remember that this journey is not just about professional advancement but also about personal growth and building more meaningful relationships in all areas of your life. Embrace these tools, engage with the exercises, and watch as your emotional intelligence reshapes your path to success.

CALL TO ACTION
Implement Your EQ Toolkit

Now that you've explored the diverse tools and resources for enhancing your emotional intelligence, it's time to put theory into practice.

This week, select one tool from this chapter that resonates with your current professional challenges or goals.

Commit to using this tool every day, whether it's starting an emotional journal, engaging with an EQ app, or participating in a mindfulness exercise.

At the end of the week, reflect on how this tool has impacted your interactions and emotional awareness at work.

Share your experiences and insights with a colleague or mentor and discuss how you can further integrate EQ practices into your daily routines.

Remember, the journey to mastering EQ is continuous, and each small step contributes to significant professional and personal growth.

CONCLUSION: MASTERING PROFESSIONAL INTELLIGENCE

Conclusion: Mastering Professional Intelligence

As we close the final pages of "Professional Intelligence: EQ for Workplace Success," we reflect on the powerful journey through the rich landscape of emotional intelligence (EQ). This exploration has not only underscored the pivotal role of EQ in the modern workplace but has also equipped you with the essential skills to transform your professional interactions, manage stress effectively, lead with empathy, and navigate your career with greater clarity and confidence.

The Transformative Impact of EQ

Throughout this book, we've seen that EQ does more than just enhance individual careers; it has the potential to revolutionize entire organizations. By mastering the art of emotional intelligence, you're not just improving your own life; you're setting a standard for those around you. Imagine being the leader who not only meets targets but also cultivates a workplace where people feel valued, understood, and motivated. That's the kind of leader EQ can help you become.

We've explored how EQ allows professionals like yourself to handle complex interactions and challenging situations with grace. Whether it's steering a team through tight deadlines, managing a heated meeting with poise, or motivating a diverse group of individuals, EQ is your invaluable companion.

Strengthening Leadership with EQ

Effective leadership is about more than giving orders and making decisions. It's about connecting with your team on a human level, understanding their needs, and guiding them through challenges not just as employees but as people. Leaders who embrace EQ promote environments where trust, respect, and open communication are the norm, not the exception.

Consider the example of a leader who used EQ to identify signs of burnout in his team. By addressing this early and realigning workloads, he not only prevented potential fallout but also boosted the team's morale and productivity. This proactive approach is what sets emotionally intelligent leaders apart.

EQ and Resilience in Times of Change

Change is a constant in the professional world, whether it's technological advancements, market shifts, or internal restructuring. Professionals equipped with EQ are better prepared to adapt to these changes. They face challenges not with fear, but with the resilience and adaptability that EQ advances.

Take the case of a manager who led her team through a major transition. By employing her EQ skills to manage her own reactions and support her team emotionally, she turned a potentially disruptive situation into a success story, demonstrating how EQ can be a critical asset in managing change.

Enhancing Team Dynamics with EQ

No professional is an individual entity, and the success of any organization depends on the effectiveness of its teams. EQ is a key ingredient in building stronger, more cohesive teams that can tackle complex projects and achieve great results. It enables team members to understand and manage not only their own emotions but also those of their colleagues, leading to improved collaboration and performance.

Looking Forward: The Increasing Relevance of EQ

As we look to the future, the importance of EQ will only continue to grow. In an increasingly automated and digital world, the human touch provided by EQ will become more crucial than ever. It's the skill that will differentiate the leaders of tomorrow, enabling them to inspire loyalty, drive change, and innovate in ways that machines cannot replicate.

Your Call to Action

As you step forward from this book back into your professional life, carry with you the principles and practices you have learned. Continue to develop your EQ through ongoing practice, reflection, and learning. Encourage your organizations to prioritize EQ development and use your skills to influence and lead with emotional intelligence.

This book is just the beginning of your journey with EQ. Continue to build on the foundation you have created here and let your growth in EQ propel you to new heights in your career. Let EQ be your guide to not just surviving in the workplace, but thriving in it, creating not only a successful career but a fulfilling one.

Final Thoughts

Thank you for joining me on this journey through "Professional Intelligence: EQ for Workplace Success." I hope that the insights and strategies shared have ignited your passion for further development in emotional intelligence. May your continued journey be rich with success and satisfaction as you harness the power of EQ to enhance not only your professional life but also your personal interactions.

Share Your Thoughts: Leave a Review

Thank you for joining me on this journey through "Professional Intelligence: EQ for Workplace Success." I hope you have found the strategies and insights provided within these pages both enlightening and actionable, and that they serve you well in your pursuit of professional and personal growth.

If this book has helped you in any way, please consider sharing your experience by leaving a review on Amazon. Your feedback not only helps us improve but also assists others in discovering the transformative power of emotional intelligence. Let's help more professionals achieve success and satisfaction in their careers!

Simply scan the QR code below to visit the book's page and leave your review.

Thank you once again for your time and engagement.

www.ingramcontent.com/pod-product-compliance
Lightning Source LLC
Chambersburg PA
CBHW070352230526
45471CB00006B/2534